Basic Cursive Handwriting Practice

PLAIN

and

not

so

PLAIN

ACADEMY

A simpler approach to
home based schooling

To the home educator,

I am very happy that you have chosen to purchase our products. We believe that our world is way too complex and that it can be simplified to avoid the chaos and confusion. Learning at home should be an enjoyable time between you and your child. Not something that they dread because they have hundreds of repetition problems to do over and over again. Plain and not so Plain Academy's approach to schooling is to concentrate on the basics and then fill in with real life learning. This approach to schooling is meant to take the stress and fear out of teaching your child at home. Your child's entire elementary schooling is going to be one big repetition, year after year. We take all the extra complexities out of schooling and get back to the basics of reading, writing, and arithmetic. By approaching schooling this way, your child will be more confident as they work through the worksheets. This allows extra time to pursue other areas of interest.

This book allows for 120 days of cursive writing practice. I would recommend doing one page per day, four times per week. As your child becomes more confident in cursive writing, you can choose to have them write their lessons in cursive. I have included 25 blank pages for extra writing practice. Make sure that your child can correctly print all letters before attempting this book. My recommendation would be to begin in third grade but if you have an older child who has not done cursive, then these lessons will benefit them as well.

Be blessed,

Amy Maryon
founder and owner of www.plainandnotsoplain.com a simpler lifestyle in our complex world

a a a a a a aaaaaaa

a a a a a a

a a a a a a

ℓ ℓ ℓ ℓ ℓ ba ab ab

B B B B B B

Abab

CCCCC

ccccccccccc

Bach Abca Cab cab

D D D D D D

d d d d d d $ddddd$

Bacd   Dad   cab   Abad

$\mathcal{E}\ \mathcal{E}\ \mathcal{E}\ \mathcal{E}\ \mathcal{E}$

$e\ e\ e\ e\ e\ e\ eeeee$

Cabe Dad bead dead

$\mathscr{F}\,\mathscr{F}\,\mathscr{F}\,\mathscr{F}\,\mathscr{F}$

$f\,f\,f\,ffff$

face   bed   cab   feed

G G G G G G

g g g g ggggg

beg face Gabe bed

Write your own A B C D E F G and abcdefg

$\mathcal{H}$ $\mathcal{H}$ $\mathcal{H}$ $\mathcal{H}$ $\mathcal{H}$ $\mathcal{H}$ h h h $hhhh$

head cab dead begged face

had had bad bad cab cab

l l l l l i i i i iiiii

bid bad fib cab abcdefghi

abcdefghi abcdefghi

A B C D E F G H I

$\mathcal{J}$ $\mathcal{J}$ $\mathcal{J}$ $\mathcal{J}$ $\mathcal{J}$ j j j j $jjjjj$

Jac   jag   did face had

I add 1 +2=3.

write all the capital letters from A-J and lower case from a-j

K K K K K K k k k kkk

Jack had a cab.

Abe feed a bead

abcdefghijk

L L L L L L l l l llll

A Lab dog had a bead.

abcdefghijkl   lkjihgfedcba

A B C D E F G H I J K L

M M M M m m m m m

Mabel a mad bird.

abcdefghijklm　mlkjihgfedcba

A B C D E F G H I J K L M

n n n n n n n n n n nnn

nab call ball lamb all

abcdefghijklmn

Write the word: call , bad, bed, life, man, gill, fib

O O O O o o o ooo this needs to go straight across at the top

Abe can mop.

Dan can land.

loop and land

PPPP p p p pppp

pan and man can land

abcdefghijklmnop

fab man can band call

2 2 2 2 q q q qqqq

queen quack Quack Queen

abcdefghijklmnopq

ball fall jam bam can

ABCDEFGHIJKLMNOPQ

R R R R R r r r rrrrrr

Rab ran far.

ear hear fear dear

lop pop mop nor for and

S S S s s s sssss

Sam is a man.

sock soap hope rope

jab cab dad mad pad

$\mathcal{T} \mathcal{T} \mathcal{T} \mathcal{T} \mathcal{T}$ t t t t ttttt

$\mathcal{T} \mathcal{T}$ $\mathcal{T} \mathcal{T}$ ft Tim

Mom has a footlong dog.

Dad has a bad car.

U U U U U u u u uuuuuu

Sam can run and hop.

Up and flip

The bee is three.

$\mathcal{V} \ \mathcal{V} \ \mathcal{V} \ \mathcal{V} \quad v \quad v \quad v \quad vvvvv$

The van is hot.

Mark is fun, so is Abe.

abcdefghijklmnopqrstuv

W W W W w w wwww

We are the light of God.

Jesus being the cornerstone.

love joy peace patience

X X X X x x x x x xxxx

exhibit   trail   river

Put on the armor of God.

Put on the armor of God.

You are loved by Christ.

Y Y Y Y y y y y yyyyyyy

Put on the armor of God.

That you may be able to stand

against the schemes of the devil.

sword of the Spirit

Z Z Z Z Z z z z z zzzzzzz

Put on the armor of God.

That you may be able to stand

against the schemes of the devil.

sword of the Spirit

belt of Truth

shoes of peace

helmet of salvation

Stand firm! Ready in your armor.

Be strong in the Lord

and in the strength of His might.

Put on the armor of God.

That you may be able to stand

against the schemes of the devil.

Helmet of salvation

Breastplate of righteousness

Belt of Truth

Shield of Faith

Shoes of Peace

Armor of God

Helmet of salvation

Breastplate of righteousness

Belt of Truth

Shield of Faith

Shoes of Peace

Be strong in the Lord

and in the strength of His might.

Put on the armor of God.

That you may be able to stand

against the schemes of the devil.

The fruit of the Spirit is

love, joy, peace, patience, kindness

goodness, faithfulness, gentleness

and self-control.

The fruit of the Spirit is

love, joy, peace, patience, kindness

goodness, faithfulness, gentleness

and self-control.

The fruit of the Spirit is

love, joy, peace, patience, kindness

goodness, faithfulness, gentleness

and self-control.

The fruit of the Spirit is

love, joy, peace, patience, kindness

goodness, faithfulness, gentleness

and self-control.

Now to him who is able to do far

more abundantly than all that we

ask or think, according to the power

at work within us.

Ephesians 3:20

Now to him who is able to do far

more abundantly than all that we

ask or think, according to the power

at work within us.

Ephesians 3:20

Now to him who is able to do far

more abundantly than all that we

ask or think, according to the power

at work within us.

Ephesians 3:20

Now to him who is able to do far

more abundantly than all that we

ask or think, according to the power

at work within us.

Ephesians 3:20

For God so loved the world that He

gave his only Son, that whoever

believes in Him should not perish

but have eternal life.

John 3:16

For God so loved the world that He

gave his only Son, that whoever

believes in Him should not perish

but have eternal life.

John 3:16

For God so loved the world that He

gave his only Son, that whoever

believes in Him should not perish

but have eternal life.

John 3:16

For God so loved the world that He

gave his only Son, that whoever

believes in Him should not perish

but have eternal life.

John 3:16

...and you will know the Truth and

the Truth will set you free.

John 8:32

...and you will know the Truth and

the Truth will set you free.

John 8:32

...and you will know the Truth and

the Truth will set you free.

John 8:32

I am the light of the world.

Whoever follows me will not walk

in darkness, but will have the

light of life.

John 8:12

I am the light of the world.

Whoever follows me will not walk

in darkness, but will have the

light of life.

John 8:12

I am the light of the world.

Whoever follows me will not walk

in darkness, but will have the

light of life.

John 8:12

I am the light of the world.

Whoever follows me will not walk

in darkness, but will have the

light of life.

John 8:12

The thief comes only to steal and

kill and destroy. I came that they

may have life

and have it abundantly.

John 10:10

The thief comes only to steal and

kill and destroy. I came that they

may have life

and have it abundantly.

John 10:10

The thief comes only to steal and

kill and destroy. I came that they

may have life

and have it abundantly.

John 10:10

The thief comes only to steal and

kill and destroy. I came that they

may have life

and have it abundantly.

John 10:10

The thief comes only to steal and

kill and destroy. I came that they

may have life

and have it abundantly.

John 10:10

It is more blessed to give

than to receive.

Acts 20:35

It is more blessed to give

than to receive.

Acts 20:35

It is more blessed to give

than to receive.

Acts 20:35

It is more blessed to give

than to receive.

Acts 20:35

It is more blessed to give

than to receive.

Acts 20:35

In all these things we are more

than conquerors through him

who loved us.

Romans 8:37

In all these things we are more

than conquerors through him

who loved us.

Romans 8:37

In all these things we are more

than conquerors through him

who loved us.

Romans 8:37

In all these things we are more

than conquerors through him

who loved us.

Romans 8:37

May the God of hope fill you with

all joy and peace in believing,

so that by the power of the Holy

Spirit you may abound in hope.

Romans 15:13

May the God of hope fill you with

all joy and peace in believing,

so that by the power of the Holy

Spirit you may abound in hope.

Romans 15:13

May the God of hope fill you with

all joy and peace in believing,

so that by the power of the Holy

Spirit you may abound in hope.

Romans 15:13

May the God of hope fill you with

all joy and peace in believing,

so that by the power of the Holy

Spirit you may abound in hope.

Romans 15:13

May the God of hope fill you with

all joy and peace in believing,

so that by the power of the Holy

Spirit you may abound in hope.

Romans 15:13

Fight the good fight of faith.

Take hold of the eternal life to

which you were called and about

which you made the good confession

in the presence of many witnesses.

1 Timothy 6:12

Fight the good fight of faith.

Take hold of the eternal life to

which you were called and about

which you made the good confession

in the presence of many witnesses.

1 Timothy 6:12

Fight the good fight of faith.

Take hold of the eternal life to

which you were called and about

which you made the good confession

in the presence of many witnesses.

1 Timothy 6:12

Fight the good fight of faith.

Take hold of the eternal life to

which you were called and about

which you made the good confession

in the presence of many witnesses.

1 Timothy 6:12

Fight the good fight of faith.

Take hold of the eternal life to

which you were called and about

which you made the good confession

in the presence of many witnesses.

1 Timothy 6:12

Now faith is the assurance of things hoped for

the evidence of things not seen.

Hebrews 11:1

Now faith is the assurance of things hoped for

the evidence of things not seen.

Hebrews 11:1

Now faith is the assurance of things hoped for

the evidence of things not seen.

Hebrews 11:1

Now faith is the assurance of things hoped for

the evidence of things not seen.

Hebrews 11:1

Now faith is the assurance of things hoped for

the evidence of things not seen.

Hebrews 11:1

Hello, my name is

My address is:

My birthday is:

Practice writing other family names:

Months of the year

January

February

March

April

May

June

July

August

September

October

November

December

Months of the year

January

February

March

April

May

June

July

August

September

October

November

December

Months of the year

January

February

March

April

May

June

July

August

September

October

November

December

Days of the week

Sunday

Monday

Tuesday

Wednesday

Thursday

Friday

Saturday

Days of the week

Sunday

Monday

Tuesday

Wednesday

Thursday

Friday

Saturday

Days of the week

Sunday

Monday

Tuesday

Wednesday

Thursday

Friday

Saturday

What is the weather like today?

What is the name of the day?

What is your name?

What state do you live in?

What is your favorite food?

What is the color of your:

pencil? _____

shirt? _____

eyes? _____

hair? _____

dog? _____

drink cup? _____

floor? _____

car? _____

What is your favorite:

game?

book?

subject?

friend?

snack?

hobby?

weather?

animal?

Copy a few lines from a book you are reading:

Copy a few lines from a book you are reading:

Copy a few lines from a book you are reading:

Copy a few lines from a book you are reading:

Write a thank you letter for a gift you received.

Write a friendly letter to a friend you miss.

Write about what you did this weekend.

Write what you want to do for your birthday.

List your top ten favorite movies:

Write some words that describe you: (ten)

What chores do you like to do the best?

What chores do you like to do the least?

Write the title of a book you are reading:

Who is the author:

What date was it published

Name a character in the story

Would you recommend this book to a friend?

Why or why not?

What activities can you do in the summer

What activities can you do in the winter

Write the names of 10 living things

Write the names of 10 non-living things

Copy the letters of the alphabet. Have your teacher mark any th
at need improvement.

aaaa

bbbb

cccc

dddd

eeee

ffff

gggg

hhhh

iiii

jjjj

kkkk

llll

mmmm

nnnn

oooo

pppp

qqqq

rrrr

ssss

tttt

uuuu

vvvv

wwww

xxxx

yyyy

zzzz

Any letters you missed or need improvement on,

write a few words with the letters that need help.

Copy the letters of the alphabet. Have your teacher mark any that need improvement.

Aa   Bb

Cc   Dd

Ee   Ff

Gg   Hh

Ii   Jj

Kk   Ll

Mm   Nn

Oo   Pp

Qq   Rr

Ss   Tt

Uu   Vv

Ww   Xx

Yy   Zz

Name ten southern states

Name ten northern states

Name the 7 continents

Name the oceans

What are the four directions on a map

Write the names of your family members

Name five places you would like to visit

What are you looking forward to the most this

summer?

Describe your dream day...

Name ten things that make you smile

Name ten things that make you sad

Write a letter inviting a friend to church

Write a letter to a person who did something nice for you yesterday.

Write the books of the Bible--new testament

Use the following pages for extra practice writing. Included is the letters at the top of the page to make it easier for those that may have forgotten how to write them.

a b c d e f g h i j l m n o p q r s t u v w x y z

A B C D E F G H I J L M N O P 2 R S T U V W X Y Z

a b c d e f g h i j l m n o p q r s t u v w x y z

A B C D E F G H I J L M N O P Q R S T U V W X Y Z

a b c d e f g h i j l m n o p q r s t u v w x y z

A B C D E F G H I J L M N O P Q R S T U V W X Y Z

a b c d e f g h i j l m n o p q r s t u v w x y z

A B C D E F G H I J L M N O P Q R S T U V W X Y Z

a b c d e f g h i j l m n o p q r s t u v w x y z

A B C D E F G H I J L M N O P 2 R S T U V W X Y Z

a b c d e f g h i j l m n o p q r s t u v w x y z

A B C D E F G H I J L M N O P Q R S T U V W X Y Z

a b c d e f g h i j l m n o p q r s t u v w x y z

A B C D E F G H I J L M N O P Q R S T U V W X Y Z

a b c d e f g h i j l m n o p q r s t u v w x y z

A B C D E F G H I J L M N O P Q R S T U V W X Y Z

a b c d e f g h i j l m n o p q r s t u v w x y z

A B C D E F G H I J L M N O P Q R S T U V W X Y Z

a b c d e f g h i j l m n o p q r s t u v w x y z

A B C D E F G H I J L M N O P Q R S T U V W X Y Z

a b c d e f g h i j l m n o p q r s t u v w x y z

A B C D E F G H I J L M N O P Q R S I U V W X Y Z

a b c d e f g h i j l m n o p q r s t u v w x y z

A B C D E F G H I J L M N O P Q R S T U V W X Y Z

a b c d e f g h i j l m n o p q r s t u v w x y z

A B C D E F G H I J L M N O P Q R S T U V W X Y Z

a b c d e f g h i j l m n o p q r s t u v w x y z

A B C D E F G H I J L M N O P Q R S T U V W X Y Z

a b c d e f g h i j l m n o p q r s t u v w x y z

A B C D E F G H I J L M N O P Q R S T U V W X Y Z

a b c d e f g h i j l m n o p q r s t u v w x y z

A B C D E F G H I J L M N O P Q R S T U V W X Y Z

a b c d e f g h i j l m n o p q r s t u v w x y z

A B C D E F G H I J L M N O P Q R S T U V W X Y Z

a b c d e f g h i j l m n o p q r s t u v w x y z

A B C D E F G H L L M N O P 2 R S T U V W X Y Z

a b c d e f g h i j l m n o p q r s t u v w x y z

A B C D E F G H I J L M N O P Q R S T U V W X Y Z

a b c d e f g h i j l m n o p q r s t u v w x y z

a B C D E F G H I J L M N O P Q R S T U V W X Y Z

a b c d e f g h i j l m n o p q r s t u v w x y z

A B C D E F G H I J L M N O P Q R S T U V W X Y Z

a b c d e f g h i j l m n o p q r s t u v w x y z

A B C D E F G H I J L M N O P 2 R S T U V W X Y Z

a b c d e f g h i j l m n o p q r s t u v w x y z

A B C D E F G H I J L M N O P 2 R S I U V W X Y Z

a b c d e f g h i j l m n o p q r s t u v w x y z

A B C D E F G H I J L M N O P Q R S T U V W X Y Z

a b c d e f g h i j l m n o p q r s t u v w x y z

A B C D E F G H I J L M N O P 2 R S T U V W X Y Z

$a\ b\ c\ d\ e\ f\ g\ h\ i\ j\ l\ m\ n\ o\ p\ q\ r\ s\ t\ u\ v\ w\ x\ y\ z$

$A\ B\ C\ D\ E\ F\ G\ H\ I\ J\ L\ M\ N\ O\ P\ Q\ R\ S\ T\ U\ V\ W\ X\ Y\ Z$

Made in the USA
Monee, IL
23 July 2020